Don't Become an Entrepreneur If…

Adrena Martin-Tolbert

Don't Become an Entrepreneur If…

Adrena Martin-Tolbert

Atlanta, Ga _____

www.whoisadrena.com___

creationzfad@gmail.com

Printed in the United States of America

ISBN:13: **978-1511644310**
ISBN-10: **1511644311**

It is in your greatest struggle that you find the most strength.

-Adrena Martin-Tolbert

CONTENTS

ACKNOWLEDGEMENTS

Before I proceed with the rest of this book, I would like to first give all thanks to God, who has been there throughout my life journey, and looked out for me on so many occasions. I would like to thank my parents who have definitely been there to support me spiritually, mentally, and most importantly financially, throughout my entrepreneurial journey. I want to thank my husband for always being supportive of my ideas, no matter how crazy they may seem, and supporting me every step of the way. I definitely can't forget all of my other family and friends out there. Anyone that has ever bought any of my products, or attended any of my events, thank you.

Remember, the best is yet to come…

PREFACE

For every action, there is an equal and opposite reaction. When something is stuck and you want to move it along, what do you do? The obvious answer would be to move it along, but what if it doesn't move? How long will you keep pushing until you finally give up? As an entrepreneur, your journey will be like that object that is stuck, and you can't seem to get going. As soon as it seems like you get 2 steps ahead, you take 3 steps backward. Eventually you get tired of pushing, but the question is, how bad do you want it to move? How bad do you want your business to be successful? For some people their business is ran like a hobby. They push at it when they can, or when they feel like putting in the work. For others they eat, sleep, and breathe their business, pushing at it every chance they get. They understand that one day all of their pushing is going to pay off.

"Don't become an entrepreneur If"…is just a list of things that I have learned so far on my 3 year entrepreneurial journey. I am nowhere near where I want to be, but I have definitely come a long way from where I started. This book is for all the aspiring and current entrepreneurs, or just anyone looking for encouragement on this journey called life.

THOUGHTS

Every action was once a thought. Some of us think fast, and take action off the first thing that comes to mind. There are others that like to take their time, and fully think something out before putting it into action. At the end of every chapter in this book, there is a page that says "My Thoughts." I want you to use this page and take a little time to write down your thoughts after reading each chapter. Write down how you feel at the time, future plans, goals, what you need to improve on, and any other thoughts you might have on your entrepreneurial journey. You never know, you might even think of a new business idea, while you are reading!

Think about, put it on paper, and get to WORK.

Let me introduce you to Ashley and David. Ashley and David are 2 young recent college graduates that have been friends since they were about 5 years old, and attended the same church. Ashley comes from a low income area with her 2 parents, and David comes from a middle class area with his 2 parents. See the difference between Ashley and David was not just their area codes, but their household conditions. Although Ashley lived in a not so desirable area, she was still surrounded by a loving family who took care of her, and did the best that they could to give her a better life. Her parents had been married for the past 20 years, took her to church every Sunday, and pushed her to be the best woman she could. David on the other hand, had a much different family structure. Yes he grew up in a nice neighborhood where his parents had plenty of money, but his family structure was a broken one. There were many mornings where he woke up to screaming and yelling from his parents. There were also many nights when he would come home, and not see his father for 5 days straight, leaving him and his mother all alone.

The one thing Ashley and David did have in common was their plans to one day both become entrepreneurs. They even talked about going into business together one day, but just wasn't quite sure what type of business they wanted to open up. Not only that, but David's parents were not that supportive of his dreams, so he made sure to keep his plans between him and Ashley. What type of business if any, will Ashley and David eventually open up? How will they survive through their entrepreneurial journey? What will their family think of what they are trying to do? Keep reading to see how their journey and struggles all pan out.

1. DON'T BECOME AN ENTREPRENEUR IF YOU ARE AFRAID TO BE BROKE

"Did you hear what was coming to town next month?" David asked excited.

"No what?" Ashley asked.

"Only the biggest event to hit the city of Chicago. All types of rappers, singers, and a bunch of other celebrities, will be in the building. They say tickets are selling out fast, so we need to go ahead and get them today." David said.

"Hmm how much are the tickets" Ashley asked. "Just $150 right now, but in a few days they are going to be more" he told her.

"Just $150 WHAT!! Do you know what I could do with that type of money right now!" she yelled. Since David's family pretty much always had money to give him whenever he needed it, he didn't have a problem going out and getting things he wanted. He could simply ask his dad, whenever he was home, or slip it out of his mom's purse, when she was hung over on the couch. It was nothing for him to spend $150 for an event ticket. On the other hand, with Ashley, money was very hard to come by, especially for something like that. Throughout high school and college, she always kept a job, just to have spending money of her own. She was also currently working up a business plan to start her pet store company, which she had decided to do a few months back.

"Ok how about this. I can get the ticket for you so we can both go together, and you can just pay me back whenever you get the money?" David suggested.

"Yes I guess we can do that, but I still think that's a lot of money to be wasting on some people, who probably make more than that in seconds." she said, shaking her head at him. Later that night David went home, only to find his mother yet again passed out on the couch from drinking too much. It was a usual for her so he was used to it. Just like he usually does, he found her purse to get enough cash to pay for the two tickets he was going to purchase later that night, and found nothing. He even looked on her nightstand upstairs to see if she had left anything up there, and found nothing again. He then got on the phone with his dad to try and get some money, and found out some shocking news. Their once lavish lifestyle was soon about to come to an end. His dad informed him that all of their life savings had been depleted and spent on an investment deal that went wrong. He wasn't sure if they would even be able to keep the house they were living in because there would not be enough money coming in to cover all the bills. They were going broke, and for the first time in his life, David knew the feeling of not having enough. Later that night he called Ashley to update her on his latest family news.

"Ashley guess what, I'm broke!" David yelled.

"Well, welcome to my world!" she laughed.

"No seriously we are going broke. I just talked to my dad and he told me we may even lose the house" he said

"And I'm serious too, I grew up broke my whole life, which is why I am trying to save as much money as I can to start my own business. I know this is new to you, but trust me, you will be fine. I guess you will just have to go get a job like the rest of us common folk!" she laughed.

David sighed.

"Yes I guess you are right, I don't know about all that getting a job stuff, but I will figure something out." he exhaled.

It sucks being broke. Especially when it's something you're not used to being. I grew up as the only child in a middle class income family. My parents are divorced, but they are both still very much a part of my life. Some people think that being the only child automatically means that I'm spoiled. Now of course being an only child has its perks, but I still had to work for things I wanted. I get my entrepreneurial spirit from my mom, who was always into some form of business, whether it being Mary Kay, selling hats, or insurance. I get my work ethic from my dad, who would always tell me that I didn't need something out of the store. As a teenager, we expect our parents to provide for us and get us anything we want. Now my dad is what I used to call cheap. If it wasn't on the clearance rack, or yellow dot sale, I didn't need it. The fact that I couldn't get something that I really wanted, is what really motivated me to go to work and make my own money. Since the age of 16, I have always had a job. Yes I blew my first paycheck, but only because I was so excited to have my own check, that I didn't know what to do with it. I had no bills, no car, or any other responsibilities to take care of. From then on I realized the power of money, and how I could control supplying my material wants and needs.

Fast forward 10 years later from that 16 year old teenage girl, and here I am, a young female entrepreneur. When I first started my business, I didn't have a budget or an investor to come in and help start me up. I would just take a little money from my paychecks and start buying jewelry supplies a little at a time. In 2013, I started doing various vending events in an effort to expand my business and get my name out. In 2014, I begin to host my own events. Initially when I started doing events, I did them in an effort to promote my brand. Since I was already traveling to Atlanta, I decided to try my luck and started doing events there. I wasn't from Atlanta, nor had any connections there, so it was hard getting started in the event field. One thing I have definitely learned about events is that it's all in the name. People support people they know, or at least believe they know through social media. My job was to make myself known in a city, where so many people were doing the exact same thing I was.

Then in April 2014, I did an event in Chicago At the time, I had partnered up with two other women, and we all agreed to split the cost of doing the event three ways. Our very first event we did together in Atlanta went well (my very first event hosting period), so we decided to take it to another city where all three of us had family. From the beginning of the event, our expenses were way more than we could handle, but we decided to try it anyway. Well to make a long story short, that three way split ended up being one way. Guess who ended up being the lucky one to take that on? You guessed it, me! I heard about every excuse in the book, as to why certain things couldn't happen, but I was determined to finish what I started. The guest left with a great experience, and I left with an empty bank account. I was pissed that the money that I had worked so hard to save up, was all gone within the course of 2 days. That has got to be the most stressful event I have ever done. Although I could have let that stop me, I kept going. I lost a lot during that time, but that was definitely a learning experience for me. Thank God my parents were able to help me out with the last little bit of funds I needed for the event, but the fact of the matter was that my savings account was gone. My husband and I drove back home from Chicago to Alabama, and as crazy as it sounds, I begin to plan my next event. As an entrepreneur, I was determined not to let my current financial situation hold me back.

ASK YOURSELF:

1) WOULD I STILL WANT TO PURSUE MY BUSINESS IF I WOKE UP ONE MORNING WITH AN EMPTY BANK ACCOUNT?

2) AM I OK WITH MAKING THE FINANCIAL SACRIFICES AND ADJUSTMENTS TO MY LIFESTYLE?

MY THOUGHTS

_____
_____
_____
_____
_____
_____
_____
_____
_____
_____
_____
_____
_____
_____
_____
_____
_____
_____
_____
_____
_____

2. DON'T BECOME AN ENTREPRENEUR IF YOU ARE AFRAID TO BE ALONE

"How are your business plans coming along?" David asked.

"It's ok, I'm just trying to get up enough money for all the supplies I need. What about you? You still broke over there!" Ashley joked.

"Haha! But yes our situation is still the same from last week. I thought about the whole getting a job thing, but I'm not sure if that is something I really want to do. I also been thinking about our little business we use to always talk about getting, what do you think?" David asked.

"I mean, I'm still interested but what are you thinking about doing, because you know I've already starting making plans for the pet supply business. Are you interested in that?" she asked.

"Hmm I don't know, possibly, but you know pets have never really been my thing. Plus I don't know, my parents keep talking to me about the corporate world, and working for one of those Fortune 500 companies. Now don't get me wrong, I know the money is good and all, but that's just not what I want to do for the rest of my life. My dad feels like he was able to afford us the lifestyle we had before, from working one of those fancy corporate jobs, so I should do the same. I just wish things were the way they were before." he said, resting his face in his hands.

"Well what are you going to do? I mean I know you don't want to go to work, but at the end of the day, you still have to live, and things have to get paid. I told my parents about the pet business and for the most part they are really supportive. They can't really help me out with much, but it's ok. These two jobs I have are coming in real handy. It's kind of hard not getting any financial support, but I will be ok." Ashley said.

"So what about your other friends, have you told any of them about your business?" he asked.

"I told a few of them, and for the most part, they all sound like your parents. The idea sounds good, but to them it's just a big waste of time. You know most of my friends live in the same area as me, and have the same financial situation, so they think the only way to make it, is to get a 'good job'. I said I wasn't going to talk to anyone else about it just because I already know what they are going to say." she told him.

"Yes, that's what I keep hearing about, this good job, and how it will make you lots of money, especially with a college degree, but I don't want to just make lots of money. I want to be rich. From what I have been reading on the internet, the millionaires in the world are all business owners, and not just employees", David told her.

"Exactly", Ashley said, "which is why I am working as hard as I do. The people around me might not see it now, but it's cool. One day I will make them a believer."

Believe In Yourself

As an entrepreneur, you will find that many people don't understand the life you live. Friends, family, and sometimes even your own spouse. When I say that you can't be afraid to be alone, I mean that both physically, and mentally. As the only child, and a newcomer to the Atlanta area, I didn't have any female friends to go to any events with. It usually ended up being me and husband at all the networking events. One of the things I hate the most when planning vendor events is when people ask me "How many other vendors do you have signed up?" That question bothers me for two reasons. Number one, it shouldn't matter how many other businesses are going to be somewhere. If your goal is to network, get your brand out, and make money, then that's all that should matter. Who cares if you are the only business there? That actually gives you more of a spotlight for your brand, so use it to your advantage. Number 2, to me that shows a sign of weakness. If you always need someone else around to validate you or your business, then that's a problem. As an entrepreneur you have to be strong enough to stand on your own in a room full of 50 people, just like you would in a room of 2.

Now let's get into the part about being mentally alone. When you are in high school about to graduate, the next step that everyone talks about and puts so much emphasis on is going to college. Why do you want to go to college? To get a good job, or at least what others think is one. All throughout my college career, we were flooded with career fairs, resume seminars, and other programs to prepare you for that dream job, probably with a Fortune 500 company. For a lot of my peers, this was their reality, after all Tuskegee University is a school that produces greatness, and nothing less within its students. For me it was no different. I graduated and could have gotten one of those nice jobs with a decent salary, but that wasn't for me. No matter how many career fairs I attended, and job interviews I went on, I just wasn't feeling it. Instead of working my resume, I would rather do research on You Tube, learning how to make various jewelry products and legalizing my business structure. When I graduated from college in 2012, I continued to be a waitress at the hotel on campus, where I had worked for the past three years. My mom would ask me all the time, "When are you going to get a real job?" Her definition of a real job, was a position in an office, or at one of those Fortune 500 companies. Now I wasn't making an enormous amount of money, but with no kids, combined with the few other income streams I had coming in, I made enough to support myself. Those jobs gave me the flexibility to still work, make money, and still work on my business goals at the same time. Even a few of my friends were either going back to school for their master's degree, which I thought about for a second, or getting good jobs. I am proud of all my friends for the path they chose, but that just wasn't mine. A lot of people didn't understand my dreams, and why I made certain moves, but pretty soon they will see that it was all worth it.

ASK YOURSELF:
1) AM I OK WITH BEING ALONE
ON MY ENTREPRENEURIAL
JOURNEY?

2) WILL I BE OK IF NO ONE ELSE
BELIEVES IN MY DREAMS?

MY THOUGHTS

_____
_____
_____
_____
_____
_____
_____
_____
_____
_____
_____
_____
_____
_____
_____
_____
_____
_____
_____
_____
_____
_____
_____

3. DON'T BECOME AN ENTREPRENEUR IF YOU ARE AFRAID OF GAINING NEW FRIENDS

"The Clash: Shopping Expo and Networking Event," was the latest headline in the newspaper Ashley read one Saturday morning. The shopping part sounded fun, but what the heck was networking, she thought. She continued to flip through the paper, and eventually landed on the internet to figure out exactly what this event was all about. She researched networking, and realized that this would be a great way to get out and meet other entrepreneurs, and hopefully someone that could help her with her pet business. Excited, she called David to see if he wanted to come to this event with her.

"David guess what!" she yelled.

"What's up?" he asked.

"I just saw an ad for this big shopping and networking event coming to Chicago in a few weeks, and guess what, it's free!" she told him.

"Ok the shopping part I get, but what about this networking half, what is that all about?"

he asked.

"Well I looked it up online and from what I understand it's a good way to get out and meet new people, especially other entrepreneurs. This can be good for us to get out and talk to other people who are already doing what we want to do." Ashley told him.

"Meet new people, no I'm all good on that. I think I have enough people in my contacts taking up space already." he said.

"Yes but the people you know are not trying to do what we are doing. Half of the people you know dropped out of high school, and still riding around doing nothing, so yes you do need to meet some new people." she told him.

"Yea yea yea, whatever! I mean we can try this little networking event, but I don't need a whole bunch of people all in my business, I already have enough stuff going on as it is." David said.

"I'm not saying you have to go and be friends with everybody, but just have a little conversation with them, and see what they do. I may even try to get some business cards made before we go, just so people can have my information to stay in touch." she said.

"Ok, well like I said, we can go, but if something crazy happens, I'm blaming you!" he joked.

"Yea and I also want you to thank me when something good comes from this also!" she joked back.

Don't Be Afraid

Now I'm not one for having a bunch of new friends either, but I think when the Drake song "No New Friends" came out, people took that to a whole new level. Don't believe the hype or the music. Trust me, that artist has made plenty of new friends to get to where he is today. As an entrepreneur, you have to be open to letting new people in. Now letting new people in does not mean they have to be all up in your personal space, but as a business owner, you have to establish some type of working relationship. As hard as it may be, you have to learn to trust people with your business. This is something that I am still working on even until this day. You feel like you have a certain type of relationship with your friends for so long, and no one else is welcomed in. Well that is what networking is all about. As the saying goes, your network determines your net worth. Since

I was a newcomer to the city and business scene of Atlanta, I relied solely on networking to help me along. Social media, specifically Instagram became my best friend. I would sit on Instagram at 3 o'clock in the morning, and email various boutiques about carrying my custom jewelry and accessories line. On top of the many trips I took from Alabama to Atlanta being a part of various networking events, my network was growing slowly but surely. Even to this day, I am still in contact with some of those same customers and vendors I met from previous events.

I think a lot of people feel like because they have done something for so long, they should continue doing it, even if it is wrong. Just because you have been friends with someone since preschool does not mean you have to continue that friendship, especially if it is not conducive to your current lifestyle. Some people are so stuck on the "no new friends" phrase that they let old friends hold them back from making progress. If you aspire to be a successful entrepreneur, then you have to hang around like minded people. Your friends that are comfortable with their 9-5 gig won't understand your lifestyle as an entrepreneur. Not to say there is anything wrong with these people, but the mind of an employee and the mind of an entrepreneur work in two different ways. An employee won't understand the late nights, long hours, low funds, and other sacrifices that go along with being an entrepreneur. So yes still keep those friends around, but you want to make sure that you are also surrounded by people that think like you. People that think like you can better understand those times when you feel like giving up. Those time when you have $0 in your bank account, but keep on doing what you are doing. What about those times when you don't have a clue about how something will work out, but you try it anyway. Entrepreneurs understand each other. Well let me rephrase that and say "Real entrepreneurs understand each other."

One thing I have learned on my entrepreneurial journey is that everyone that starts a business, and claims to be an entrepreneur, isn't who they say they are. Some people get the impression that starting a business is easy. They think that they can simply come up with an idea, buy some products, promote a few times, and that's it. When it comes down to it, they don't really have what it takes. They want the entrepreneur perks, but don't want to do what it takes to get them. This is why having new friends is so important. Especially for those people who have friends that aren't doing anything with their lives. If they haven't made anything of their life, what makes you think they will be happy to see you do something with yours? If anything you may just have to distance yourself for some time to get your mind right, and eventually go back to those friends and be an inspiration to them. Moral of the story: You need new friends!

ASK YOURSELF:
1) AM I OKAY WITH SEPARATING
   MYSELF FROM CERTAIN
   PEOPLE THROUGHOUT PARTS
   OF MY ENTREPRENEURIAL
   JOURNEY?

2) AM I OPEN TO RECEIVING NEW
   PEOPLE INTO MY LIFE?

MY THOUGHTS

_____
_____
_____
_____
_____
_____
_____
_____
_____
_____
_____
_____
_____
_____
_____
_____
_____
_____
_____
_____
_____
_____
_____
_____

4. DON'T BECOME AN ENTREPRENEUR IF YOU ARE AFRAID TO LOSE SLEEP

"David, do you know what time it is? Wake up so we can get ready to go to this event!" Ashley yelled to David through his voicemail. This was the day they were supposed to be going to the big shopping and networking event in Chicago. Two hours later he finally called her back and she was pissed.

"Hey Ashley my bad, I overslept and didn't realize you called me earlier." he told her.

"Your bad, really David? What the heck are you so tired from anyway, you didn't do nothing all day yesterday." she said.

"Yes, but you know Saturday is the weekend and that's my time to rest." David said.

"REST! David you just told me a week ago that your parents were going broke, you don't have time to rest. I mean unless of course you are ok being like that". she told him.

"Yea Yea, I know, I'm still getting used to this myself. What time is the event over, maybe we can still make it out?" he said.

"It ends in about 30 minutes, but by the time we get in the car and sit in traffic it's going to be over. Next time I'm going without you. What else do you have planned for today?" she asked him.

"Well I was thinking of maybe going out looking for some jobs, and really thinking more about this business I want us to open. Then of course get a few more hours of sleep." David told her.

"See there you go talking about all this sleep again. I'm going to look online and see if there are any other events going on we could go to. In the meantime get up and get yourself together. Oh yea, how are your parents doing, have things gotten any better between them?" she asked him.

"Things definitely haven't improved. My mom is still drinking like a fish, and my dad is always gone. I'm still trying to figure out exactly what he is doing to be gone so much. I mean the way he explains things, you would think he was working for the FBI or something. I know my mom is just drinking because of him, but I need to do something to help take her mind away." David told her.

"That would be nice, but where and how? " she wondered.
"I haven't figured all of that out yet, but I'm

thinking of something" he said.

"Well whatever it is you figure out, you won't get it done in your sleep!" Ashley joked. If we want to at least be a little successful, we are going to have to start making certain sacrifices, and one of them is sleep. No more sleeping in until 1pm, even if it is on a Saturday." Ashley told him.

"Ummm ok, I'll see what I can do about that one!" he joked back.

"Yes you will!" she laughed.

Dream Big

Sleep is the one thing you seem to never have enough time for. As an entrepreneur the feeling is only intensified. As hard as you try to get a few hours of sleep or even a nap in, there is always something else for you to do. There have been plenty of times when I will be tired, and I will tell myself that I would just go and lay down for a few hours. Instead of actually going to sleep, I either end up on Instagram or thinking of my next business move. My sleep pattern is pretty weird. Well, then again I think it has been for a while now, dating back to my college years. I'm the type of person that will call myself "taking a nap", at 12am, then wake back up at 3am and be full of energy. Now back in college, getting sleep was a little easier because I could easily just get out of class, and go to my dorm and sleep until it was time for me to go to work. I miss those days! The days when life was easy. The days when all I really had to worry about was going to class, and keeping my grades up. Nowadays it's a whole different story. The more I try to sleep, the more things I find to do.

Along with money and friends, sleep is another one of those things that you have to sacrifice in order to be successful. They say the early bird catches the worm, which is definitely something I have learned on my entrepreneurial journey. You can't sleep half the day away, and still expect to get the same things done had you gotten up early. We always say there are not enough hours in the day to get things done. Well starting your day off early will definitely help out with that. If you are someone who has a hard time getting up in the morning, start small. Get up maybe 15 minutes earlier than usual, then eventually move to 30 minutes and so on. Personally if I sleep past 9am, I feel like I have wasted part of the day. Usually my cats wake me up every morning for food at about 5:30am. At 5:30 I don't want to be bothered, but of course I end up getting up and feeding them. I might stay up and work on a few things depending on how I feel. Then I might sleep for another 2 hours until it's time to get up for work or class. Even in that short span of time, there are a lot of tasks that I can accomplish. Make every second count! Another way to utilize the most of your time is to make use of your idle time. Idle time for me is riding in the car with someone while they drive, or at a friend's house waiting on them so we can leave. Even something as small as posting on social media, which surprisingly takes longer than you might expect if done correctly, can be done in idle time.

Do your research and study the habits of other millionaires. I can almost guarantee you that the majority of them are up before the sun comes up. Like I said, I am still a work in progress with this one. My dad even calls me really early in the morning, and I usually miss his calls because I am still in the bed. Early in the morning is also a good time to run errands, and clear your head, I guess because the majority of the population is still sleep, which gives you an advantage. One thing that I am also working on is starting each morning with prayer, and reading the Bible. I watched my mom do this all while I was in high school. She would get up early in the morning, and come downstairs and sit on the couch. I asked her what she was doing, and she told me she was praying, and reading her word. She would also get up and cook breakfast, and the rest of dinner for the night. These are definitely great habits to pick up on, ones that will surely make a huge difference in your life. Now don't get me wrong, going too long without getting enough sleep can be damaging to your health, but just with everything is life, there has to be balance, and change. You may not be able to get your full recommended hours of sleep each night, but you can make it up in other ways. You may be working an important project for a client, or yourself, that requires you to spend a few extra hours up than usual. Or if you are like me, and always have a million ideas going through your head, it may be hard to get sleep even when you feel like that is what you need to do. It's all a part of the sacrifice and hustle of being an entrepreneur.

Moral of the story: Don't be afraid to lose sleep! The small sacrifices you make today, will definitely pay off in the long run. You will lose sleep as an entrepreneur, but it's all a part of

the process, and one of the sacrifices you have
to make on the way to success.

ASK YOURSELF:
1) AM I READY FOR A LIFESTYLE OF LATE NIGHTS AND EARLY MORNINGS?

2) AM I READY TO ADJUST MY SLEEP PATTERNS FOR MY NEW ENTREPRENEURIAL LIFESTYLE?

MY THOUGHTS

_____

_____

_____

_____

_____

_____

_____

_____

_____

_____

_____

_____

_____

_____

_____

_____

_____

_____

_____

_____

_____

_____

_____

5. DON'T BECOME AN ENTREPRENEUR IF YOU ARE AFRAID OF REJECTION/CRITICISM

"Hello David, did you bring a copy of your resume with you?" the job recruiter asked David.

"No sir I didn't, I wasn't aware that I needed to bring one." David replied.

"You were unaware that you needed to bring a resume to a job interview. I believe my assistant spoke with you yesterday to confirm, and told you the specific things to bring." the recruiter told him.

"I'm sorry I must have missed that part yesterday. Is there any way I can bring it to you later on?" David asked him.

"My schedule is pretty booked later on, so how about I just keep your resume on file and call you if something else becomes available." the manager told him.

"Ok thank you." David told him before he shook his hand and walked out the door. When David had gotten almost out the office door, and to the hallway, he saw the manager rip his application up and put it in the trash.

"Well I guess he won't be calling me after all" David said to himself.

The next week David went on a few other interviews, and this time he bought his resume with him. Only this time the problem was that he didn't have enough experience for the job he applied for, so he never got a call back from that either. Feeling defeated, David called Ashley to tell her about what had been going on with him.

"Ashley, am I a failure?" David asked.

"A failure? No why would you ask that? she asked.

"Because I can't get a job. For the past two weeks I have went on a number of interviews, and keep hearing the same thing, 'we will give you a call back, thank you for coming in.' I mean, Jesus Christ what do I have to do beg and plead with them to hire me on?" he explained.

"David just because you haven't gotten a job this far does not mean you are a failure. Did you ever sit back and ask yourself what you may have done wrong in the interviews, and why they didn't call you back? Were you dressed right? Did you answer the questions right? Were you even fully prepared for the

Interview in the first place? she asked.

"Well to be honest, no I didn't. I just assumed that since I had a college degree, I would be a good candidate for any job I put in for." he told her.

"See that's the problem, you assumed. I mean think about it. Look at how many people have a college degree out here and still don't have a job. If having a degree made it that easy, the unemployment rate wouldn't be what it is. So answer those questions now. Were you prepared? Were you dressed right, and how were your communication skills?" she asked.

"No, no, and no! I mean I looked good, but I could have done better in the other two areas." David said

"Well, there you go! You can't just go around blaming someone else, and you don't have your own self in order. Ashley said.

"Yea you're right, I guess I'll go and try this job hunt again before I go crazy over here. I NEED SOME MONEY!" David yelled.

"Me and you both!" Ashley said.

"What is the latest with the pet business, have you made any progress yet?" he asked.

"You know, just when I thought I did, something else always comes up. You know in life when you think you have it all figured out, you realize that you don't. I was looking up pricing and distributors yesterday, and I didn't realize how expensive some of this stuff can get. I may need to think about doing something else." Ashley said.

"So you just going to give up like that!" David asked her.

"Now you know giving up is not in my blood, I was made for this!" she laughed.

Rejection is something that we all face. No matter where we go, or what we choose to do in life, there will always be some form of rejection. You definitely shouldn't even think of becoming an entrepreneur if you are afraid to handle rejection. We may not see it at first, but rejection is one of those things that make us stronger. Rejection helps us build character and also realize certain things about our brand. I remember setting up as a vendor at my very first networking event. I drove all the way from Alabama to Atlanta to set up and sell my products and didn't make not one dime. I mean people would stop by and look, and tell me how cute my items are, but they weren't selling. I was a little pissed off at first, especially considering what I invested into this trip (money, gas, etc.), but I used that as learning lesson. It really made me pay attention to other jewelry business products that were selling and really figure out what I was doing wrong. See my problem was that I had been catering to one market for so long with my products, that business wise I wasn't ready for a bigger one like Atlanta. Another problem I had is that I would just sit in my room creating jewelry that I liked, but not necessarily what other people wanted to purchase. I mean I thought my designs were cute, and anyone would be crazy not to want them, but I was wrong. As I really sat back and analyzed my products in comparison to my competition, I realized that my products looked cheap. I even had someone tell me that, but I thought they were tripping. Even though all my products were handmade, that doesn't mean they have to look as such. I had gotten used to just creating those cheap pieces and selling them for $5-$6 in a small town, but it was now time for a change. I had to put my big girl panties on and realize that if I wanted to compete in the big leagues, I had to step my game up.

Some people may feel like because someone didn't verbally say something about their products or brand, then they like them. What people fail to realize is that no reaction can be the biggest reaction of all. Especially with people that don't know you. Instead of them criticizing us like a friend would, they just simply won't buy from you. This is why when I come up with a new design, especially something that I know may be a little out of the box, I have to show a few of my close friends to get their opinion. I already know that I have a wild imagination so I just want to be sure that what I created is something that people will actually wear.

Now you definitely have to learn the difference between constructive criticism, and someone forcing their ideas upon you. Good criticism will actually build you up, and help you better your brand. Good criticism will not just be subjective to how they think something should be done. As I stated earlier on, along with jewelry designing, I also plan various events as well. Naturally after each one of my events, I like to get feedback from the guests, and participants of the event, just so I know what I can do to improve for next time. Well I made the mistake of asking one guest in particular what they thought. In addition to criticism of the event, I begin to hear their subjective comments on what they personally didn't like and would have done differently. So because you don't like fruit punch, I should have had orange soda. Or because you don't like white walls, the walls should have been red. Little things like that, have nothing to do with anything, but just your opinions of what I should have done differently. That bothered me for a minute, but then I remembered that everyone else had nothing but positive things to say about the event. I realized that it's not me, but them, this was my event not anyone else's. That's the one thing I had to learn about criticism, you can't please everybody. No matter how good you do something, there will always be those one or two people to find something wrong with it. I guess you just have to watch what you ask for, especially if you are just starting out. As a new business owner, you will be really vulnerable. You will be vulnerable to opinions, competition, and anything else someone has to say about your brand. Only through trial, error, and research will you really gain the confidence in your brand to not let the little things bother you.

Moral of the story: Don't be afraid of rejection and criticism. Learn from it, and move forward. Eventually you will learn the difference between constructive criticism, subjective ideas, and hate.

ASK YOURSELF:

1) AM I READY TO DEAL WITH REJECTION?

2) HOW WILL I HANDLE NOT ONLY REJECTION OF MYSELF, BUT MY BUSINESS AS WELL?

MY THOUGHTS

_____

_____

_____

_____

_____

_____

_____

_____

_____

_____

_____

_____

_____

_____

_____

_____

_____

_____

_____

_____

_____

_____

_____

6. DON'T BECOME AN ENTREPRENEUR IF YOU ARE AFRAID OF FAILURE

"Drum roll please. And the winner is… Karen Sanders." the host announced. Ashley had just entered into a pitch contest that was held in the city every six months. This was a contest for young entrepreneurs to pitch their business to local investors, who were willing to invest a certain amount of money into their startup company. She had been planning for this for the past few months, and thought for sure she had a chance of winning at least something. Later that evening she called David to tell him about the contest and the results.

"DAVID I LOST! I mean I planned for months and thought for sure I had a good shot at something. I even told a lot of our church members and friends that I was doing this and had a good chance of taking home the prize. Now what do I tell them?" she asked him.

"You tell them the truth. Tell them you did your best but you just didn't win this time. I'm pretty sure this won't be the last time you get a chance to do something like this. I know how bad you wanted this, but it's ok, there is always next time. And besides, what about all that talk before about asking yourself why things happen the way they did, did you answer those questions yourself?" he asked.

"Yes, kind of. But I just feel like such a failure. It's just like all my hard work went in vain. I know there is a next time, but I wanted to win this time." she sighed.

"It's ok. I mean, I'm pretty sure you aren't the only one who failed at something like this at first. You know I've been doing a little research on my own, and I found out that a lot of the celebrities, and popular businesses we know today, had a lot of failures in the beginning. It's what made them who they are today. You never know what may come from this." David told her.

"That sounds convincing, I just need to get that through my head and stop beating myself up about it. On another note, how is the job search coming, did you get something yet?" Ashley asked him.

"Yes finally! I start training on Monday. It took me long enough but I finally got something." he told her.

"That's great! Did you tell your parents yet?" She asked him.

"I did. My dad was happy, and told me I can

start helping out with some of the bills around the house. My mom was happy as well, but she was more concerned about borrowing money from me to go and get booze. She hasn't worked in years, so with one income, she was just depending on my dad for money. The less he comes home, the less money she gets. He makes sure all the bills were paid, but for the most part that's it. My mom had gotten used to just being a housewife for so long, that it's hard for her to get up and get a job. She pretty much just sits at home and drink all day." he explained.

"Wow that's sad I didn't know it was that bad. Well maybe you can encourage her to get up and do other things. I mean you never know what is going on in her head. She may just be depressed about your father." Ashley told him.

"Yea you're right, I'm going to start spending more time with her and get her back on her feet. I WILL NOT LET HER FAIL!" he said.

In our lifetime, we will all fail at something at least once. No matter how hard we try to avoid it, it will happen. Failure is just like rejection and criticism, they are there to teach us a lesson. Back in 2013, a year after I had started my business, I was growing impatient and wanted to try something that I thought would make me a few quick dollars. No I didn't start selling drugs or any other illegal activity, but I begin to sell hair. The hair care industry is a billion dollar industry. It's an industry that I decided to try my luck with, in hopes of making some quick sales for my business.

There was a particular housewife from a show, who had just started a hair extension company. At the time, I was all into the whole "find a celebrity to get on" phase. I thought that by selling a celebrity endorsed product, I could surely increase my sales by a great deal. So I proceeded to sign up for the most expensive starter package deal they had, which included bundles of hair, entry into the hair show, conference calls with the housewife, and a list of other things. I was excited about starting this new venture, and begin promoting on social media, and to all of my other friends and family. Business was slow, I mean real slow, but I'm glad that it was. Sounds crazy, but my mom was my very first and only customer that I had with the hair. What she received were cheap, bad quality bundles of hair. To make a long story short, that whole business deal was a complete waste of time and money.

I'm not even sure if that particular housewife was even really involved with the company. It seems as though they were just paying to use her face and name for branding. Bad decision. I never officially told people that I was done selling the hair, but when they asked, I just told them I was not into that anymore.

When you first fail at something, you may feel a sense of embarrassment that you were not able to succeed at what you set out to do, but then you have to realize that everything happens for a reason. I definitely learned a valuable lesson from that experience. All of the time and energy that was spent trying to sell hair, I could have put that same energy and into my jewelry business. I was looking for a quick fix to a problem that can only be resolved with hard work and dedication.

My experience with failure didn't discourage me, or keep me from moving forward, but it only made me a better businesswoman. Some people fail one time and some people fail 100 times, until they finally get something right. No matter how old you are, you have experienced failure at some point in time of your life. You don't just fail in business, but in many areas of your life. There are failed relationships, friendships, classes and many other things. Even as a baby when we first tried to stand up and walk, we fell because we were not developed enough to stand. No matter how many times we tried, we would not fully be able to stand until it was the right time. As a truly dedicated, driven entrepreneur, who is passionate about their business, a little failure won't scare you off. No matter how hard you fail, if something is in your heart and you are determined to see it through, a little failure won't hold you back.

One of my biggest inspirations for dealing with failure would have to be the story of Tyler Perry. This is a man that had a dream, and spent his last dollar trying to make it happen. This is a man who spent his entire savings account producing a play, only to have a few people show up. This is a man who slept in his car for some months, until he was able to get back on his feet. Tyler Perry went from being a homeless man on the street to a millionaire. Now if that doesn't inspire you to keep going, I don't know what will. The fact that he overcame failure and turned his negative into a positive shows his determination, and drive to be successful. Moral of the story: Failure is there to make you strong. Even though we may not see or realize it, there is a lesson that comes from each failure. And just remember that everything and everybody comes into your life for a reason, season, or lifetime.

ASK YOURSELF:

1) HOW HAVE I OVERCAME MY
FAILURES IN THE PAST?
2) AM I READY TO HANDLE THE NEW
FAILURES THAT COME WITH BEING
AN ENTREPRENEUR

MY THOUGHTS

_____

_____

_____

_____

_____

_____

_____

_____

_____

_____

_____

_____

_____

_____

_____

_____

_____

_____

_____

_____

_____

_____

_____

7. DON'T BECOME AND ENTREPRENEUR IF YOU ARE AFRAID OF COMPETITION

"1, 2, 3, 4, 5, oh my goodness! I didn't know there were so many other pet supply companies out there. I mean I knew I wouldn't be the only one, but I didn't know there were so many already on the market." Ashley said. Her and David had been up all morning researching different companies in their field.
"So, what does that mean!?" David joked.
"It means that it's going to be that much harder for me to get my business out there. Why would someone want to invest in something that there are already so many of?" she asked him.
"Well that is your job to tell them why they should invest. If that was the case why would anyone else ever want to start a business? I can almost guarantee you that just about anything you can think of has already been created." he told her.
"So what do you suggest I do?" she asked him.

"Umm I don't know, be creative! Use that brain of yours and come up with something." he laughed.

"So you got jokes now!" she laughed.

"Of course! No but seriously I heard about another one of those networking events that is coming to town next week, and this one is geared towards Veterinarians, kennels, and anyone else in the pet industry. I think it would be a good idea for you to go, maybe even bring some of those business cards you said you were getting printed." David explained.

"Sounds like a plan! How much is it, because you know I'm working with limited funds here?" Ashley asked him.

"This one is only $10, I'm sure you can do that!" he said.

The next week they went to the event and actually got there at a decent time, thanks to David getting up on time. When they got there, Ashley was even more amazed as to the amount of people and vendors that were set up. She just couldn't get over all the other entrepreneurs who were already doing what she wanted to do.

"It looks like I have some serious work to do." she told David.

"Of course! I told you just have to be creative. Just like there are hundreds of fast food restaurants and every other type of business in the world the same thing goes for the pet business. People love their animals!" he told her.

"Yes I know. Let's get out of here and get something to eat. By the way have you thought anymore about what business you want to open up? You think you want to join me in the pet business?" she asked him.

"I don't know about all the pet stuff, but I was thinking of us doing some type of graphic design company or something. You know that I've always had a thing for art." he told her.

"Well let's make it happen!" Ashley told him.

Competition is everywhere. Everywhere you turn, and everywhere you look, competition is there. Some people are so afraid of competition, and try to stay as far away from it as possible. If you want to be a successful entrepreneur, you have to embrace competition. When I first started making jewelry, I studied my competition just to see what type of pieces they were making. I wanted to know how their designs compared to mine. So when I would go to various events an set us as a vendors, I wanted to be far away from other jewelry tables as possible. I had the mindset that if I was too close to someone selling the same products as me, I wouldn't get any sales. What I failed to realize was the power of branding. I was so busy worrying about the competition and them out selling me, that I wasn't focused on my brand. The problem with a lot of entrepreneurs is they focus so much on just having a business, and not on building a brand. The difference between a business and a brand, can be the difference between success and failure. See the thing about a business is that everybody has one. Anybody can go to the store, buy some products, and start selling them. Anyone can think of an idea for a service, and start offering it to people. It takes a lot more work and planning to successfully build a brand. A brand is something that people equate with a certain quality, feeling, taste, or look. When I think of the McDonalds brand, I automatically think of the Golden Arch. The Golden Arch is a symbolic sign that you are either at, or in close proximity of a McDonalds. I also think of low cost fast food. When I think of the Louis Vuitton brand, I think of a high quality, luxury accessories brand. What do people think of when they hear your business name? Do they just hear the name of a business that has certain products, or is it a recognizable brand. When people hear the name CreationZ From A Dove, I want three things to come to mind: 1) handmade, 2) creative, and 3) unique. I pride myself on having one of a kind statement designs. This also correlates with my events. I want them to remember that in addition to creating jewelry, I can create, plan, and execute quality networking events. I use the motto "Where creativity and fashion collide" That saying holds true for everything I do, whether it be designing jewelry or planning events. When people see the CreationZ From A Dove logo on anything, they should already know what to expect.

Even when I am signing up vendors for events, most of them want to know how many of a certain type of vendor will be there. They want to make sure that their chance of competition is as low as possible. I mean if you are the only clothing boutique at an event, everyone will come and shop with you right? Wrong! Even if you are the only boutique in a room full of 100 people with only a few other vendors, if you do not have what they want, they will not shop with you. This is why it is so important to brand yourself and figure out your target market, and what it is that they are purchasing. Personally, I don't care how many other jewelry designers will be attending an event, because at the end of the day, no one has jewelry like mine. I am confident in my product and what I have to offer my customers, so it does not bother me. If people are not shopping with you, then it is up to you as a business owner to figure out what the problem is .I think that is another problem with new entrepreneurs, they don't want to work. They want the perks of being an entrepreneur, but don't want to do what it takes to be successful. This is why so many entrepreneurs fail, because they let their competition out due them. One of the business definitions I will always remember from one of my college classes is "the art of outdoing your competition, knowing that your competition is trying to out due you. Life is a competition. It is a game that with the right moves, you have a winning chance at. Moral of the story: Embrace competition. Competition is your friend, and will put you on the path to being a successful entrepreneur.

ASK YOURSELF:

1) WHO OR WHAT ARE MY COMPETITORS IN MY FIELD OF BUSINESS?

2) HOW WILL I VIEW COMPETITION; AS A THREAT, OR AS ANOTHER WAY FOR MY BUSINESS TO BE SUCCESSFUL?

MY THOUGHTS

_____

_____

_____

_____

_____

_____

_____

_____

_____

_____

_____

_____

_____

_____

_____

_____

_____

_____

_____

_____

_____

_____

_____

_____

8. DON'T BECOME AN ENTREPRENEUR IF YOU ARE AFRAID TO LET GO OF FEAR

"Are you still working on doing the graphic design business?" Ashley asked David.

"Yes I am, I actually have a notebook filled with ideas since the last time we talked about it." he told her.

"That's good, I been thinking about it to, and I think it would be a good idea. Even with me doing the pet business I'm still going to need graphics for marketing and things like that. So what are the next steps?" she asked him.

"Well I've been talking to a few other people about it to, and I don't know, they kind of scared me a little bit." he said.

"What do you mean they scared you, what did they say?" she asked looking confused.

"I mean it wasn't anything too bad, but I talked to an older guy that used to have his own graphic design business. He told me how he had to end up going out of business, because his competition down the street had better prices than him." David told her.

"Ok and what else did he tell you?" she asked demanding.

"Nothing much. I just told him how I wanted to have my own graphic business, and he just told me to be careful, and watch out for the competition." he told her.

"So that's what got you all scared over there!" she laughed.

"You laughing but I'm serious. I know we talked about this last week, when we were talking about the pet industry, but it's not the same." David said.

"It's not the same, how is it not the same?" Ashley wanted to know.

"I mean I know that it's all about business, but you never talked to anyone with experience in that field, and I did." he told her.

"Oh so now you want to chicken out because of what somebody else told you?" she joked again.

"No I'm not a chicken I was just saying." he said.

"Look you're going to start this business and that's final. I don't want a chicken for a business partner. On another note, how is your mom doing, did you get her back on track?" she asked.

"She is doing much better, she still drinks a

little, but nowhere near as much as she used to. I even got my dad to start coming home a little more." he said.

"Well that's good, you never know she may even want to open up a business of her own one day." Ashley told him.

"I don't know about all of that now, let's just take it one day at a time!" he laughed.

"How do they feel about you being an entrepreneur now? They still on you about keeping a JOB?" she asked.

"They are more supportive than what they used to be. Maybe because I actually sat down and explained my plans to my dad, it might make a little more sense to him now. Of course I talk to my mom about it while I am there with her, and it's pretty much the same with my dad. I mean I know that I need to keep a job for now to pay the bills, but within the next few years, I want that job to be a thing of the past." David told her.

"Now that's good to hear, and just as soon as you let go of this fear, we can really get this thing off the ground. I'm ready!" Ashley said.

Don't become an entrepreneur is you are afraid

to let go of fear. Fear is the one of those things that we all have. The difference between us as humans, are the things that we fear. For instance myself, I have a fear of snakes, which I am pretty sure I am not the only one. I have never had any close interaction with a snake, but from what I see on TV and have heard from other people. This is the problem with a lot of people, they have a fear of the unknown. They have a fear of something they have never experienced before, but because someone else told them it was bad, then they want no parts of it. Now in certain situations, fear of the unknown is ok, and even makes perfectly good sense, what is called common sense, but when it comes to business, it is another thing that can make the difference between your success and failure. Now obviously if you know that something is harmful for you then you should not try it. For instance you already know that if you go too far near a cliff, you run the risk of possibly falling over. You have never experienced falling over a cliff, but common sense tells you that if you do this, something bad will happen, so don't try it. Common sense fear is ok, but what about the other not so common things we fear based on someone else's experience? Their encounter with it may have been bad, but someone else may have had a totally different experience.

There are many people who have started a business, and invested lots of money on the business, only to have it fail. Because of their failed business they begin to have a negative outlook and advice on becoming an entrepreneur. These are the people that will try and discourage anyone they know from attempting to make the same mistake they did, or so they think. They feel as though since they had one bad experience with business, they have become an expert to anyone that ask. This is where fear of the unknown comes into play for the new entrepreneur. Take for instance your Aunt Sharon. Aunt Sharon opened her restaurant business up three years ago. She started her business like all other entrepreneurs, with the goal to make money. Sharon took out business loans borrowed money from family members, and even took out a loan on her car to get her business up and running. She hired employees, had a grand opening, and took all the necessary steps to make her business successful, or so she thought. Just one year after her grand opening, she was forced to close down the restaurant. Everything she worked for and built was gone. Quite naturally, Aunt Sharon became angry, upset, and bitter. How could something she worked so hard for, be gone down the drain within just a year of business? Fast forward two years later, and here you are in the same place Aunt Sharon had been when she first started her business. You are in the beginning stages of your business, but you are unsure of what some of the next steps are, so you turn to the only person you know with a few years of experience as an entrepreneur, Aunt Sharon. Since Sharon is still bitter about her own business failing, she tells you the complete opposite of what you should be hearing as a new entrepreneur. She tells you about her experience with business, all the money she lost, and how she would not recommend anyone to be in her shoes. She then begins to try and convince you not to pursue your entrepreneurial dreams, because just like hers, your new business will fail as well. It is at this point, that you being to panic, and that fear of the unknown sets in. Since you look up to your Aunt Sharon, you take her words and conversation to heart, and start convincing yourself how bad of an idea it would be to continue on your entrepreneurial journey.

It is people like Aunt Sharon that will scare a lot of new entrepreneurs away from pursuing their dreams. They become afraid of their own business failing, and without even trying to pursue them, they lay them down for something else. What you have to realize is that, your dream was not meant for everybody. Just because something did not work for one person does not mean that it was not meant to work out for you. God did not give everyone the same vision, so you can't expect them to understand yours. By you having Aunt Sharon as your only entrepreneurial mentor, will cause you to be discouraged, and you miss out on some great opportunities with your business.

Her fear of the past, is guiding your thoughts of the future.

Get rid of that fear. As an entrepreneur you have to be willing to take risks. You have to be able to think on your feet. Yes you do want to make the best decisions with calculated risks, but sometimes, you just have to jump out there and do it. Don't let the Aunt Sharon's out there discourage you from following your dream. If something didn't work for another person, don't just take their words for face value and run with it. Instead of talking yourself out of your business because of your fear, figure out what you can do differently to make your business succeed. Instead of allowing Aunt Sharon's words to fully get in your head and alter your decision, ask her the W questions, who, what, when, where, and why? Who did she have around her at the time she started her business? Who came into her life after, and what role did they play as a part of her business? What was she doing to make her business successful? What type of marketing was she doing? Where was she focusing here promotional efforts with the store? Why did she close the business down? All of these questions along with more are what you should be asking anyone that had a failed experience with something. By asking these questions, you can get a better understanding of the business, and also learn key points to ensure your success with your business.

Moral of the story: Always do your research, and let go of the fear. Never let fear of the unknown hold you back from following your dreams.

ASK YOURSELF:
1) AM I ALLOWING FEAR TO HOLD
ME BACK FROM DOING THE
THINGS I REALLY WANT TO DO?

2) AM I READY TO COMPLETELY LET
GO OF FEAR TO FOLLOW MY
DREAMS?

MY THOUGHTS

_____
_____
_____
_____
_____
_____
_____
_____
_____
_____
_____
_____
_____
_____
_____
_____
_____
_____
_____
_____
_____
_____
_____
_____

9. DON'T BECOME AN ENTREPRENEUR IF YOU ARE AFRAID TO HAVE FAITH

"I think I like that one better" Ashley told David. He was doing the final drafts for her new business logo, and business cards. It was almost time for them both to unveil their new business ventures for the world to see. Ashley still didn't have all the funds she needed to fully start her business, and on top of that her mom had just lost her job, but she still decided to keep going with it anyway.

"With all the edits you had me do I should be charging you!" David joked.

"Yea right! That's real funny. she laughed. Anyways have you gotten any other clients so far?" she asked.

"You know it's crazy because I told a few of the members from the church about what I was doing, and about 4 of them said they need new logos for their business. I guess this graphic thing isn't so bad after all." he told her. "See what did I tell you! Once you stopped being a chicken you were able to get your whole business going. And you know with me on you team, you won't be stopping anytime soon." Ashley said.

"Of course I know, you won't even let me get my rest now! But how is the pet business coming along, did you get all the supplies you wanted for it?" he asked her.

"Not exactly. You know when my mom lost her job, that kind of set me back a little bit. The money I was using to save up for products, I had to start using it to help out with the bills. Now I'm not going to sit here and tell you I didn't think twice about even going through with this whole business idea, just because of everything that was going on. You know how it is, if it isn't one thing, it's another. I thought about waiting another year until I had more funds, but you know what, I decided to just step out on faith and go for it now. You know what the pastor always talks about in church. He says that if you have just a little bit of faith, God will do the rest." Ashley told him.

"Well I'm sure as heck glad you didn't decide to wait a whole year from now. You would've left me all along on this confusing entrepreneurial journey" he said.

"Yes I know you wouldn't have known what to do with yourself!" she joked. "How is everything at home, I'm sure your parents are proud of you?" she asked.

"Things are much better. My mom finally decided to go get a job. She even stopped drinking! She said she don't know how much longer she wants to do it, so I don't know, maybe my entrepreneurial spirit rubbed off on her, we will see. My dad is proud of me to. He comes home every night and I don't hear as much arguing like I use to. I don't have to wake up to broken glass anymore. They are even talking about going to church together and everything. It's amazing because they are the ones who got me into the church years ago in the first place. I don't know exactly what happened in between, but I'm just glad that they are working it out now." he explained to her.

"Good. See I told you everything would work out. I'm still working on my situation at home, but I'm not going to stress over it." Ashley said.

"Yea you're right, no point in stressing. I guess we just have to have faith, and let everything work itself out. I don't know what you got me into with this whole entrepreneurial thing, but I think I like it!" he joked.

"I don't know either, but I just know that one day our struggle will all be worth it. Until then let's enjoy the journey." she said.

Having faith is one of those things, that in tough situation, it is hard to do. When your $800 rent is due in three days, and all you have is $100 to your name, it is hard to listen to someone tell you to have faith. When you are in a bad relationship, and you are hoping for a change, it is hard to have faith. Faith is that intangible thing that you just have to believe that is there, and working in your favor. When we first started the process of moving to Atlanta, we didn't really have a full thought out plan as to what we would be doing once we got up her. I mean I knew I wanted to continue expanding my jewelry brand, and get more into the fashion industry, and my husband wanted to further his music career, but how? All we knew is that it was time for a change, and since we had spent so much time in Atlanta, why not move there. We had dreams and goals, and ambition to get us through. I set a date and told myself that I wanted to be moved by that particular date. One of the issues we had was our apartment that we were currently still living in. Our lease did not end until the summer of 2015, and the only way to get out of it, was to either pay off the remaining balance, or find someone to take over our lease. My husband and I both agreed to attend the Art Institute in Atlanta and felt that it would be a good move for the both of our careers. Although I had a degree from a university in Marketing, I wanted to formally educate myself in the world of fashion. We explained our new plans to our apartment complex in hopes that they would understand and let us out of our lease, but of course it didn't happen like that.

We begin the process of looking for a new tenant to come in and take over our lease. We did postings on Craigslist, put up flyers around the neighborhood, and through word of mouth. We also started to apply for different apartments in the Atlanta area. We explained to them our situation about how we were moving from out of state and wanted to get an apply solidified for our move, and they all told us the same thing, that we needed to have our name removed from our current lease in Alabama before they could help us.

Time was passing by quickly and it was getting real close to the time for us to move. I started getting nervous, and begin to wonder if it was meant for us to move in the first place. I mean, personally I felt it was time and was ready to move, but was it the right time? Was that the plan God had set up for us? We would get calls and emails from various people who were interested in the apartment, but it never ended up in our favor. They either were not qualified for the apartment, or simply didn't respond after a few days. When I set goals for something, I try my best to make sure that they are met. But one thing I had to realize is that just because I want something to happen at a certain time, does not mean that is what is supposed to happen. Sometimes our plan is not on schedule with God's plan. Like the saying goes, HE may not come when we want him, but he HE is always on time. It's crazy because just when I thought that our certain plan would not work out, it did. We ended up getting our apartment situation figured both in Alabama and Atlanta, and were able to move on our scheduled date. Yes I doubted for a minute, but in the back of my head, I always had faith that things would work out.

Faith is all about believing for the unknown. You have absolutely no clue how something is going to work, but all you can do is have faith. There are other stories I could tell you of when my faith was tested, but throughout each situation, I learned a valuable lesson. See the other thing with faith is that you have to trust both the good and the bad. Faith also requires you to put forth an effort to better the situation. Some people think that they can just ask the Lord for something, and then sit back and wait on Him to make it happen. They continue to pray and ask the Lord for things, and then get angry with HIM, when thing don't work out in their favor. When you are going through a rough situation, you have to ask yourself what you are doing to personally change your situation. Just complaining and murmuring about a situation will not change it. You have to take the first step to make the change that you want to see, and then let God do the rest. Even if things do not work out in our favor, just know and remember that everything happens for a reason. Don't get angry with God because you didn't get the promotion that you wanted at work. There is a better job waiting on you. Don't get upset when one of your business ventures fail, you were probably meant to start something better.

Moral of the story: Everything happened for a reason. Have faith, trust your struggle, do your part, and let God handle the rest.

ASK YOURSELF:
1) IS MY FAITH STRONG ENOUGH
TO GET FEAR OUT OF MY
HEAD?

2) WHAT CAN I DO TO MAKE MY
FAITH STRONGER?

MY THOUGHTS

_____
_____
_____
_____
_____
_____
_____
_____
_____
_____
_____
_____
_____
_____
_____
_____
_____
_____
_____
_____
_____
_____
_____

ASHLEY AND DAVID

The story of Ashley and David was used to show you that anything is possible. Ashley came from a two-parent household in a low-income neighborhood. Poverty was all she knew her whole life, but she refused to let that stop her from following her dreams. Her situation is actually what motivated her to start her entrepreneurial journey in the first place. She just knew there had to be a better life out there than what she had grown up with. I mean she loved and respected her parents for what they had done, but she wanted more for them.

David on the other hand had the money, nice house, and cars, but the one thing that he didn't have was his family. He wanted something that money couldn't buy, his sanity. He wasn't really used to doing much growing up, and even all through school, but when his parents almost went broke, that was a wakeup call for him to get up and make something of his life as well. He wasn't used to working for anyone else, and once he started it, he knew he wouldn't be doing that for long. It's a good thing he had someone like Ashley around him to get the idea of entrepreneurship into his head.

No matter what your situation is, there is always opportunity to grow. See the thing about opportunity is that, it doesn't just knock on your door and wait for you to decide if you want to answer. There are times when a good opportunity may come along, and we let someone else talk us out of doing it. By the time we decide to take the opportunity, it has already moved on to someone else. Well if that happens, don't sit around and talk about how you wish you could have done something, and wonder what if, get out and make another opportunity for yourself.

Entrepreneurship isn't for everyone. I mean if everyone were an entrepreneur, who would we have to help run our businesses for us? Who would work behind the counter inside of the bank that we go to make deposits? Who would we on the receiving end of our customer service calls when we need assistance with something? For those who do want to start or continue on this journey, do not let EXCUSES hold you back. You know excuses, the one thing we all make up when we don't feel like doing something, or maybe we feel like doing it, but don't have the courage to. Forget what someone did to you years ago, to hurt you. Stop worrying what this person might say about your decision. It doesn't matter that you grew up in an impoverished neighborhood, and can barely afford to buy yourself a hamburger. IT'S OK! The moment you decide to stop making excuses and let go of the past will be the moment you finally start living. And hey, even if it doesn't work out, at least you can say you tried.

THINGS TO AVOID AS AN ENTREPRENEUR
(If you want to be successful)

EXCUSES

I touched on this a little bit earlier, but if you ever want to have any type of success, not just as an entrepreneur, but life in general, you have to give up the excuses. For some people, excuses are a part of their everyday routine. They wake up in the morning making excuses, have conversations with their friends making excuses, and even go to bed at night doing the exact same thing, making excuses. How many of you have been around people like this? Every time you ask them something, it's always a reason why they couldn't get it done. "I couldn't get my homework done because I didn't have time", "I couldn't promote my business today because I had to watch my kids", and the list goes on and on. Instead of giving me excuses, I would rather have someone be honest and tell me that the reason why something isn't done is because they didn't want to do it. Not only are you being honest with me, but with yourself as well. If you find yourself always making excuses for something that you know you are supposed to be doing, it's time for you to sit down and ask yourself what the real issue is. The thing with us humans is that when we really want to do something or go somewhere, we will make time and a way to get it done. I don't care how tired you are, if you really care about the class that you have a 10-page paper due in, you will find a way to get it done. If you are like me, and have a 10-page paper to write, you will probably cram it in 2 nights before it is due (don't judge me for being a procrastinator, I am trying to do better!) At the end of the day, it gets done. If I make it a habit to promote my business via social media every day of the week, and for the next two weeks I don't promote at all, that's a problem. When my husband asks me why I haven't been promoting and I tell him because I didn't have time, yet I have done everything else under the sun within that time period, that's a problem. I would then need to ask myself why I haven't been promoting. Did I get discouraged about not getting the sales I wanted in the previous weeks? Did someone say something to me to make me not want to promote anymore? Or is this the business I want to continue to do in the first place. If this isn't what I want to do, then why continue to waste not only my time, but also someone else's, on something that doesn't make me happy. You see, when you continue to make excuses and get nothing accomplished, you will continue to get the same results, NOTHING. Do everyone a favor, and DROP THE EXCUSES!

NEGATIVITY

Stay as far away from negativity as possible! Especially as a new entrepreneur, you already have enough issues to worry about, so you don't need to have that as an added one. Negativity can come from anyone such as family, friends, co-workers, and anyone else you may encounter. For some people I think that negativity is a part of their DNA. They don't know how to be anything else but that. Negativity goes hand in hand with criticism. I'm sure you have encountered that one person, where they have something negative to say about any and everything you tell them. If you tell them it's a nice day outside, they will tell you why it's a bad day. You tell them about this exciting new idea you have for a business, and they tell you why it won't work. You tell them how good your spouse is, and they find a reason why you should leave them. Negative Nancy, and Sad Sam. Just think about it, how can you possibly accomplish anything positive if everything you hear is negative. You want to start your new business, but all you keep hearing are reasons why you shouldn't. You want to change some bad habits, but all you keep hearing are reasons why you won't last. How can you grow from that? It might be especially hard to deal with if it is coming from a close family member, like say your mom, dad, or spouse. You would think that the person closest to you would be the most supportive, but sometimes that isn't the case. A lot of times, people are negative because of something that happened to them. It could be something that happened during their childhood that they are still holding on to, or something happening in their life now. While you should stay away from these people, at least for the sake of your business and sanity, it wouldn't hurt to see about getting them the help they need. Approach with caution!

GREED

One thing you don't want to be in life is greedy. Greed and the love of money will kill you. Sure we all want to make money, but there is a right, and wrong way to go about getting it. I'm sure you have seen the stories on the news, or read about those business owners in the newspaper, who got caught up in a Ponzi scheme, or some other type of illegal scam where money was involved. What they had just wasn't enough, so by any means possible, they wanted to acquire as much money as they could.

You don't just want to go into business with the only goal of getting money. Not only will your business suffer, but your customers will suffer as well. The whole point of starting a business is to fill a need that isn't already being met in your current field. You are there to solve a problem that hasn't been solved by other business owners. If the only thing on your mind is how you can get rich, how can you focus on solving a problem? How can you listen to your customer's needs, if you have no interest in them to begin with? In my few years of being an entrepreneur, I have come across some greedy people myself. When you first meet them they seem like they are great business people, but when it comes down to it, they are all for self. Stay away from those type of people. Greed will make a person do some crazy things. Greed will cause you to forget your whole purpose of doing something in the first place. Greedy people will go to any lengths to be successful, even if it means hurting you. These are also the type of people that will use you for everything you have, just so they can get a few steps ahead of you. Now it may seem like these people are winning for a while, but at the end of the day what is done in the dark will always come to light. Another thing I learned from listening to successful people talk, is that the more you give the more you receive. Instead of being so focused on how much money you can make as an entrepreneur, focus on the bigger picture of how you can help someone solve a problem. Focus on how you can be a blessing to someone else, and the blessings will come to you. One of the previous presidents at my alma mater said that the secret to his success was that he gave, and helped others. This is a man who owned two successful businesses, and donated thousands of dollars to the university. His words have stuck with me to this day, and have really changed my way of thinking, not just in business, but life in general. Just remember, GREED WILL LEAD YOU TO HELL. If you want to be successful in this world, give more receive less, and watch your business grow.

IMPATIENCE

If you want to be successful with entrepreneurship and anything else you do in this life, you have to be patient. Nothing will happen overnight. In this new age of technology, everything is quick. We can get on the Internet and find just about anything we want within a few seconds. We can pick up our cellphones and reach our family and friends with a matter of moments. Many people have the same mindset when it comes to their business. They think they can just open up a business one month, and in the next month they will become the next Oprah or Bill Gates. What a lot of people fail to realize is that there was a lot of time and money invested into those two billionaires building their brands. There were a lot of failures before they achieved success. You have to be patient. I think a lot of people are fooled by what they see on TV as well, especially reality shows and videos. They think that because this person has on a $500 pair of shoes and drive a nice car, they have "made it" What we don't see off camera is what these people go home to. Those same people who seem to be "balling" on TV are broke in real life. A lot of the houses, cars, and jewelry we see are all rented. Those people have to keep up with a lifestyle that probably half of them can't afford. It's hard trying to be something you're not.

As I told you earlier, I used to be impatient. I wanted to do the easiest thing to make a little money, and that didn't work either. Yes it does get hard, especially when you feel like you are doing your best and don't know what else to do. It's easy to just say forget it and stop doing it altogether, or continue to make excuses for yourself. I would rather work hard and earn success, than have it given to me any day. You can't grow and learn if you have never been through anything. You wouldn't have the same appreciation for something that was just given to you versus you earning it yourself. If you started your business today and then next week you sell out, that would be awesome. I'm sure a lot of people would want that, but what lesson would you have learned from that. How will you know how to handle some of the failures that may happen after your success, if you have never dealt with them before? What about the stories of people who grow too fast? They can't keep up with the amount of business they have, because they were not prepared for it.

You might wonder how someone cannot be prepared for the business they have coming in, I mean that should be a good thing right? The problem is, they never had time to grow. Growth is what helps you develop not just in your business, but life in general.

Be patient and have faith

LACK OF FOCUS

You have to stay focused! Lack of focus is another one of the reasons why so many entrepreneurs fail, or just give up altogether. Entrepreneurship is not one of those things where you can just start it, work on it one day, put it down for 5 days, and then wonder why you aren't seeing any results. You get out what you put in. I know it may be hard, especially just starting out, but it's another one of the many sacrifices you have to make. This is why it is so important to surround yourself with like-minded people. You need people who will keep you grounded, and hold you accountable for your business success. It's easy to lose focus when everyone around you is doing the opposite of what you are doing. You know you should be working on your business plan, but everyone around you is getting ready to go to the club. You know you should be saving money to purchase new inventory, but everyone around you is out getting the latest pair of shoes and clothes. If you aren't strong enough to stay focused around the people you have with you now, then you need to start looking for a new group to hang around. You need to really sit back and ask yourself what is important to you. Are you more interested in hanging out all the time with your friends, or focused on building your brand. Now don't get me wrong, there is nothing wrong with going out and having a good time, we all need that from time to time, but not so much to the point that it distracts you from your goals. Just like a newborn baby needs nourishment to grow and stay alive, the same concept goes for your business. If you don't stay focus and pay attention to the needs of the baby, it won't receive the proper care it needs. If the baby does not receive what it needs, well then you have even bigger problems. Continue to think of your business as that newborn baby that needs to be taken care of. Even after you are out of the startup stages of your business, you still want to continue to put as much effort into your business as you did in the beginning. Don't think that just because you have reached a certain level of success that you can just slack off and continue to have that success. Do that, and before you know it, someone will have come along, knocked you off your pedestal and took your customers with them. Each day is another day to be better than you were the day before. You can never stop improving and learning. Remember this road wasn't meant to be easy, but nothing easy is worth having. Continue to remain focused and keep your eyes on the prize.

CLOSING REMARKS

After reading the last nine chapters of this book, you should now be able to determine if you are ready to become an entrepreneur. Even if you are currently doing business, my hope is that you will remain strong and continue on your journey. The road will be hard, just like anything else worth having in life. When you try and take the easy route to success, growth cannot take place. Growth comes when we rise about our failures. Think about it. How could you have effectively learned how to ride a bike, without falling off of it a few times? How would we have learned to walk without falling down a bunch of times as well? Just like we had to go through the developmental stages as a child, and even though our adult years, the same concept applies to our business. The more we fail, the more we learn, that is if we apply what learned during our failure to our everyday life. Don't be one of those people who have one bad experience, and just give up completely. One of those people, who like Aunt Sharon, become bitter after failure, and never try again. If I had given up after my many failures, and money lost, you would not be reading this book right now. It's been plenty of times when I questioned myself, and wondered if this is even what I am supposed to be doing. I wondered if I should just stick to having a job for the rest of my life, and let go of my dreams.

When you are going through a situation, all the shoulda, coulda, woulda, and what ifs start to resonate in your head. Not only do you question yourself, but you begin to question the Lord, and ask HIM why certain things happen to you. That is when I really started to realize that everything happens for a reason. Just because something does not happen when we think it should happen, does not mean that it won't happen at all. It just may not be your season. If you try to plant flowers in the wrong season, they will die. They will die because it was not their season to live. When you plant those same flowers during the right season, and in the right environment, they will thrive. Don't just look for the quickest and easiest way to success, but go through the struggles and growing pains that come with success. Yes they will hurt, but they are only there to make you stronger. Remember, it is in our deepest trouble that we find the most strength.

Be patient, Be strong, Be persistent

AFFIRMATIONS

I am GREAT
I am a FEARLESS
I am COURAGEOUS
I am CONFIDENT
I am TALENTED
I am ONE OF A KIND
I WILL NOT BE
DEFEATED
I WILL NOT MAKE
EXCUSES
I WILL NOT LET MY
PAST DEFINE ME

My Brand

Out networking and selling my products at an event back in 2014

One of my favorite pieces, my signature gold button bracelet

At another event last summer

Custom pieces from my jewelry line

The hubby
and I

For more information about myself, and my brand, visit my websites at www.whoisadrena.com along with www.creationzfromadove.com

Follow my social media platforms
as well:
Facebook- CreationZ From A Dove
Instagram- @creationzfromadove
Twitter- @creationzfad

BUSINESS RESOURCES

Business Startup
www.sba.gov

Patent/Trademark
www.uspto.gov

Copyright
www.copyright.gov

Tax ID Number
www.irs.gov

ABOUT THE AUTHOR

Adrena Martin-Tolbert is an entrepreneur, wife, daughter, and friend. She is the owner and founder of CreationZ From A Dove, which is a business that specializes in handmade jewelry and accessories. The idea of CreationZ From A Dove was conceived in April 2012, toward the end of her tenure at Tuskegee University. As a soon to be college graduate, she knew that entrepreneurship was something she could see in the near future. She also realized that she wanted to somehow break into the fashion world, creating new and exciting products, for both men and women alike. Her first product was a simple elastic bracelet, which turned into other jewelry and accessory items. Her goal for her business is to have CreationZ From A Dove in boutiques and stores across the country, and become a household name around the world.

Along with being an entrepreneur, Adrena also enjoys giving back to the community, and helping others in need, which is evident through her membership in Zeta Phi Beta Sorority Inc. She desires to one day be able to start a foundation to help other aspiring entrepreneurs receive the necessary training and funding to be successful in their field. Adrena is also making a name for herself through the planning and execution of various events. The goal is to give small businesses like her, an outlet to showcase their products and network with other people. You can look forward to seeing much more from Adrena and the CreationZ From A Dove brand.

Don't Become an Entrepreneur If…

www.ingramcontent.com/pod-product-compliance
Lightning Source LLC
Chambersburg PA
CBHW070812180526
45168CB00002B/582